W9-ACI-799

DATE DUE

1/1/97			
03/03/97			
DEC 1 2 2000			

THE LETTER FORMS AND TYPE DESIGNS OF ERIC GILL

NOTES BY ROBERT HARLING

THE LETTER FORMS AND TYPE DESIGNS OF ERIC GILL

PUBLISHED BY EVA SVENSSON AND DAVID R. GODINE

These notes were first published in
ALPHABET & IMAGE
and now, revised and expanded,
are published by
EVA SVENSSON
and printed by the
WESTERHAM PRESS
April 1976

First U.S. edition published in 1977 by
DAVID R. GODINE, Publisher
306 Dartmouth Street
Boston, Massachusetts

U.S. EDITION
LCC No. 76–24232

Hardcover ISBN 0–87923–200–5
Softcover ISBN 0–87923–201–3

U.K. EDITION
ISBN 0 903696 04 5

CASEBOUND EDITION
ISBN 0 903696 05 3

I

CONCERNING THESE NOTES

The following notes on Eric Gill's letter-forms and type designs derive from two pieces published in *Alphabet & Image*, an occasional quarterly, which James Shand of the Shenval Press and myself started in the early post-war years when it was possible for two youngish men (one preferably a printer) to start such a magazine on a shoestring, give or take an eyelet.

The pieces were written, primarily, because Gill's *Felicity* and *Joanna Italic* seemed to me two of the joys of twentieth-century type design, and, partly, because, as a typographical student, I had been fortunate enough to attend some of Gill's latterday lectures at the Central School.

Years after the lectures I visited him at Pigotts, the pleasantly familial commune which he set up near Disraeli's old home at Hughenden in Buckinghamshire, and where he started, with Réné Hague, his own printing-shop. On one of those visits, Howard Coster, that most zestful of photographers of men, also came along and took the picture of Gill reproduced here: to my eyes one of the best of all portraits of the artist, as agreeably disputatious as ever, but relaxed and thoroughly enjoying himself on his home ground.

Some months ago Rowley Atterbury of the Westerham Press suggested that these pieces might be reprinted. That suggestion has provided an opportunity to look through the text, make a number of revisions and to include several additional examples of Gill's early lettering.

Since I wrote the original pieces, the Gill bibliography has assumed impressive proportions, but two publications provide an unusually comprehensive view of the man and his work. On the personal side there is Robert Speaight's absorbing and compassionate biography, and, on the specialist side, Wolfgang Kehr's impressively exhaustive monograph, *Eric Gill als Schriftkünstler*. Still further volumes on his work as sculptor, controversialist, and the rest are plainly still to come, but those two books will suffice for all those interested in Gill as man and lettering artist.

Fortunately, ample resources await all would-be-thesis-writers, for Gill was as careful in keeping track of his work and in annotating original drawings, rubbings, proofs and photostats as any accountant-turned-archivist could desire. The amount of material at the Victoria & Albert Museum and at St Bride's Printing Library is quite prodigious. Gill's widow, Mary, was not only a generous benefactor, but a large-hearted one, too, for she included Gill's explicitly erotic drawings as well as engravings of letter-forms. They are all in the archives – on special application, of course.

A considerable amount of Gill material has also been assembled in the United States where Gill's renown lives on. This material is shared mainly between the William Andrews Clark Memorial Library of Los Angeles, and the Richard A. Gleeson Library of San Francisco. The material ranges from Gill's earliest known drawing, dating from his Brighton schooldays and reproduced on the opposite page, to the original drawings for the *Jubilee* type from the Stephenson Blake Type Foundry of Sheffield. All of which suggests that thesis-writers of the future will have to be transatlantically motivated. But Ford, Harkness, Leverhulme and the rest of the grant-providers will doubtless oblige with relevant travel warrants.

For help with the notes which follow I am indebted to several people who either knew Gill or were equally interested in his work; to his nephew, sculptor John Skelton; to James Mosley of the St Bride's Printing Library; to John Dreyfus and John Goulding of the Monotype Corporation; to Walter Tracy of the Linotype organisation; to Fairfax Hall of the Stourton Press; to Will Carter of the Rampant Lions Press; and to Eva Svensson of the Westerham Press. And the keepers of the V & A Prints and Drawings were as helpful as they always are. I am also grateful for ready response to enquiries from Steve D. Corey of the Gleeson Library, University of San Francisco, and Thomas F. Wright of the William Andrews Clark Memorial Library, University of California.

Suggested amendments or corrections to these notes will be appreciatively received and noted if sent to Eva Svensson at the Westerham Press for onward direction.

Robert Harling
1976

Railway drawing by the young Gill 1891

2

THE LETTER-FORMS

Eric Gill contended that his interest in letter-forms derived from a youthful interest in railway engines. As a schoolboy he liked to draw locomotives, and even began to think of himself as a potential engineer. Fortunately, whilst yet young, he learned that for such a career an interest in mathematics is more important than a talent for drawing. Engineering for him was doomed from that moment.

'If you are keen on engines,' Gill wrote many years later, 'you collect engine names ... and if you draw engines you cannot leave out their names.' The railway engines had LB & SCR or LMS or GWR or whatnot in large letters along the boiler. At this time lettering had hardly won 'specific

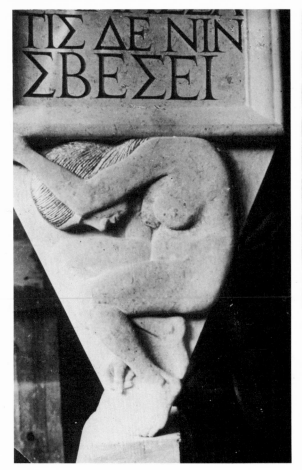

LEFT: *Gill's first carving 1910*   RIGHT: *Carving and inscription 1917*   OPPOSITE PAGE: *Brush-drawn, early 1920s*

recognition' as a subject for his especial consideration. Yet in this activity his life came full circle, so to speak, for, after his sans serif letter was standardized for use in all printing and publicity for the London and North-Eastern Railway in 1937, he was delighted to draw a wooden nameplate for *The Flying Scotsman*.

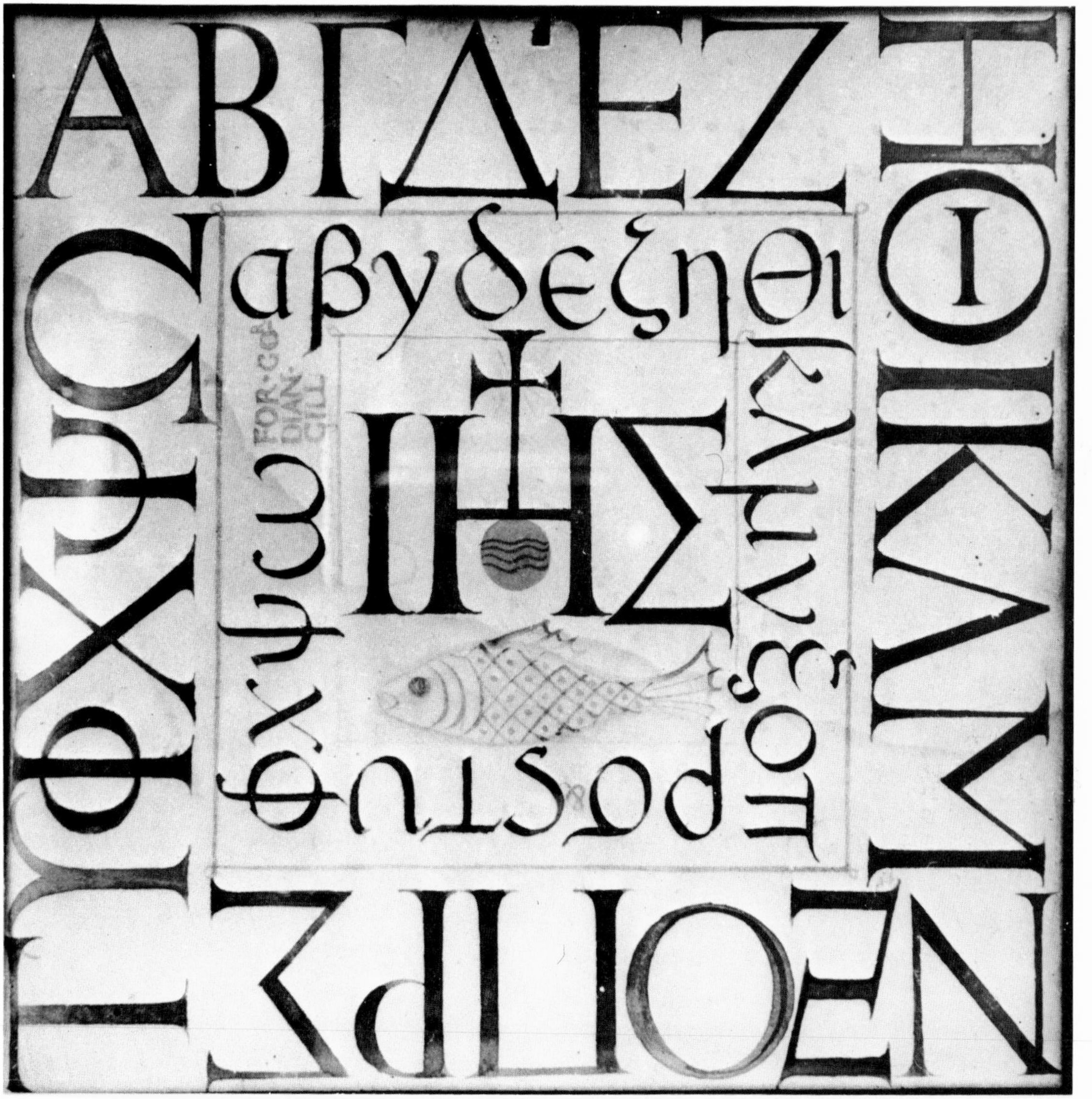
ΑΒΓΔΕΖ
αβγδεζηθι
IHΣ

Rubbing from an inscription 1915

These railway exercises took place in his early days in Brighton, before the aesthetic awakening occasioned by the Gill family's removal to Chichester. At the art school in that small cathedral town he came under the sympathetic influence of George Herbert Catt and began to discover that letter-forms were something special in themselves. Within a short time he was, as he said later, 'in a not too inaccurate manner of speaking, "mad" on lettering,' and the mania persisted.

In 1899, when he was seventeen, Gill got his first job in a London architect's office. A full account of his daily routine, frustrations and antipathies is to be found in his lively *Autobiography**, which contains clear evidence of his early determination to speak out and damn the consequences. He was out of sympathy with the commercialism of the large architectural practice in which he was the smallest unit, and he disliked the mock mediaevalism prepared so assiduously

---

*Published by Jonathan Cape, 1940.

Christmas card 1908

Three martlets 1914

Bookplate 1909

Chalice and Host 1914

Colophon 1915

Bookplate 1920

WOOD ENGRAVINGS BY GILL 1908–1920

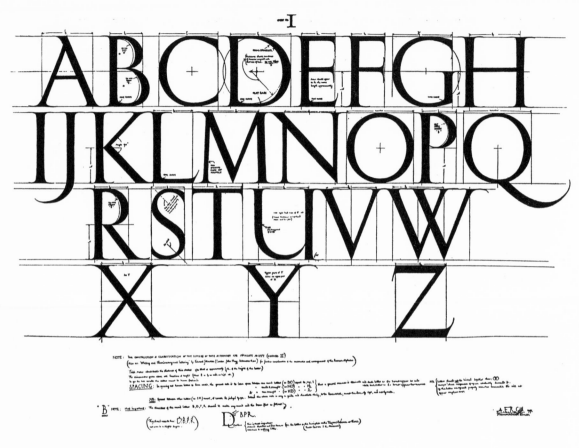

Plate 1 (half-size) of a set of alphabets drawn in 1907

and profitably in the office. He also rebelled against many other things, including his own naïvety. Yet, paradoxically, but perhaps understandably, he was happy. Within the patriarchal apprenticeship system of the drawing-office he worked hard and made friends.

His rebelliousness was partly based on his acceptance of the theories of Fabianism, so strongly in the air at the turn of the century. He would not, he protested, engage in the malevolent practices of industry, especially industrial architecture. His own theories of design were strongly func-

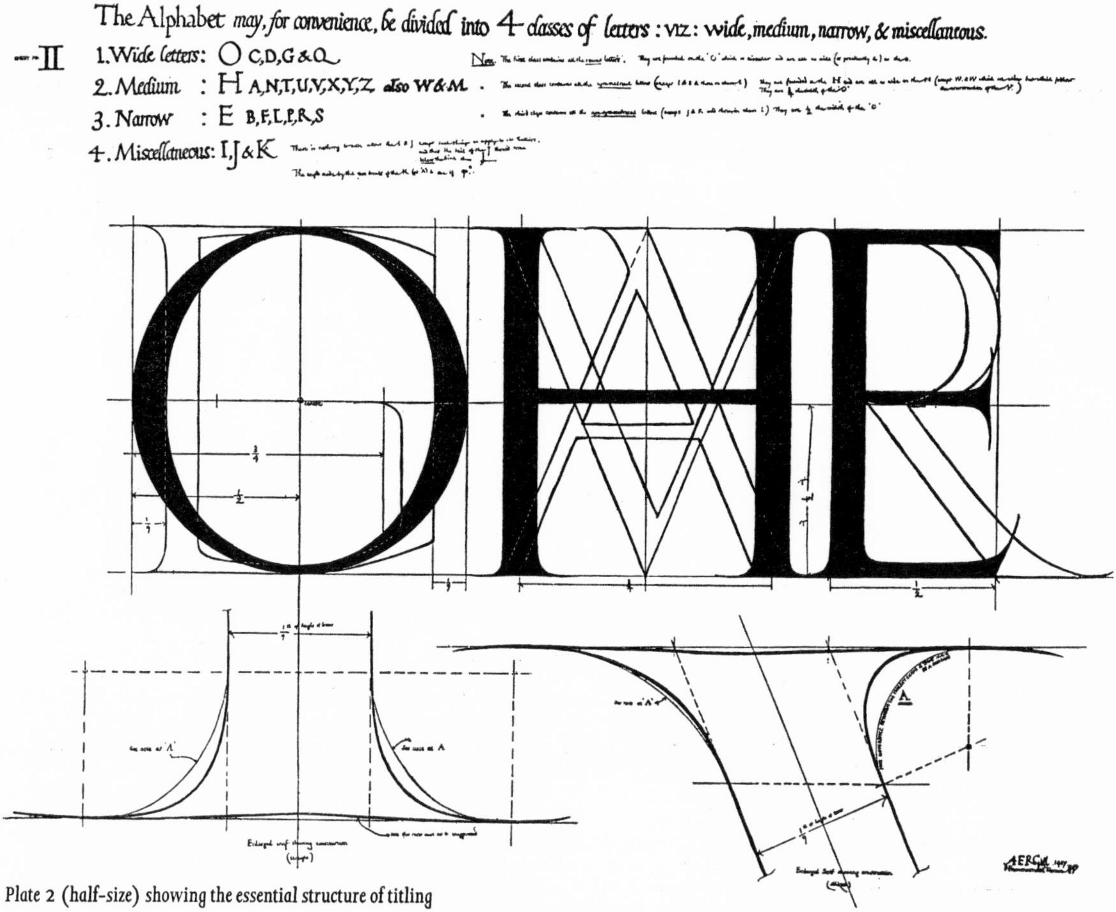

The Alphabet *may, for convenience, be divided into* 4 *classes of letters* : viz: wide, medium, narrow, & miscellaneous.

II 1. Wide letters: O C,D,G & Q
2. Medium : H A,N,T,U,V,X,Y,Z *also* W & M
3. Narrow : E B,F,L,P,R,S
4. Miscellaneous: I,J & K

Plate 2 (half-size) showing the essential structure of titling

tional, but he realised that there was little likelihood of a young man, without patronage, being able to build up a practice whilst following such theories. Even if he did and were successful he would have to employ other men, and that prospect also upset him. Altogether, he seemed determined to make a difficult future for himself.

Deliberately, therefore, if we are able to believe him – although the romantic and the realist were always nostalgic neighbours in his reminiscences – he set about learning something of

Aabcdefghijkl
mnopqrstuvw
quxyz2345678
9

Plate 3 (half-size) showing lower-case to accompany Plate 1

masonry and the craft of letter-cutting. He attended the Westminster Technical Institute where he was befriended by another teacher, George Carter. He also studied at the Central School of Arts and Crafts, then in Regent Street. His interest in lettering had persisted throughout his architectural training, and he had been responsible for most of the lettering required in the

Aabcdefghijklmn

opqqurstvwxyz

Plate 4 (half-size) showing italic forms

office. At the Central School, then under the direction of W. R. Lethaby ('who shall measure the greatness of this man?' asks Gill) that interest was to receive a vital impetus, for there he came under the influence of Edward Johnston.

The impact of Johnston's teaching and personality upon Gill was immediate, marked and lasting. 'He profoundly altered the whole course of my life and all my ways of thinking,' Gill wrote forty years on, and anyone who ever attended a lecture by Johnston, even when he was an old man, will echo Gill's tribute.

Yet Gill was also aware of the limits of his indebtedness, and was prepared to draw a line denoting those limits, a fact underlined in a letter written, a few months before his death in 1940, to Professor A. R. Hinks of the Geographical Society. 'As perhaps you know,' he wrote, 'I was a pupil of Edward Johnston and was living almost next door to him when he was designing the London Passenger Transport Board sans serif. It was a revolutionary thing and, as you know, at one go it redeemed the whole business of sans serif from its nineteenth-century corruption. It was not until 1927 that I was asked by the Monotype Corporation to do a sans serif for them. This was designed, of course, for a somewhat different purpose from that of the LPTB. The latter was designed primarily for station name-boards and only later became a printing type, whereas the Monotype sans serif was designed first of all for typography, and moreover for machine punch-cutting. It therefore seemed desirable to me that the forms of the letters should be as much as possible mathematically measurable and that as little reliance as possible should be placed upon the sensibility of the draughtsmen and others concerned in its machine facture. Thus the E has equal arms and the middle one is as near as possible to the middle and so throughout. I do not myself think there is much to choose between Gill Sans and Johnston Sans, but I do think the alterations I made might be said to be an improvement from the point of view of modern methods of production.'

Most typographers would agree with Gill's modest defence of his own sans serif, whilst deprecating his wholesale condemnation of nineteenth-century sans serif designs. Several of those anonymously-designed types are of an extremely high standard, and, in their larger sizes, as wood letters, could scarcely be improved upon for use in posters. A few were undoubtedly the models for some of the successful German sans serif designs of this century.

Throughout their long and close relationship, Johnston and Gill remained friendly. Indeed, in 1901, Gill and his brother, Max, moved from Clapham to share rooms with the master in Lincoln's Inn, testimony enough to their compatibility at that time and to Johnston's kindliness. Only Gill's later conversion to Catholicism seems to have clouded that early compatibility.

Stone-cutting probably gave Gill the aesthetic escape he needed. Also, according to the recollections of Sir Sydney Cockerell, there was a lesser-known impetus. 'I knew Eric Gill at the

INSET: *offset reproduction of alphabets by Gill chiselled in hoptonwood stone, 1909*

ABCDEFGH
IJKLMNOP
QRSTUVW
XYZ

Aabcdefghijklmno
pqorstuvvwxyz &
abcdefghijklmnopqrst
uvwxyz 1234567890

very beginning of his career as a carver of monumental lettering', he writes,* 'and then brought to his notice Hubner's *Exempla Scripturae Epigraphicae Latinae* (Berlin, 1885), which reproduces an immense number and variety of beautiful Latin inscriptions. Gill profited greatly from a study of this invaluable work and varied his lettering accordingly.'

Sir Sydney's recollection also suggests that, even at that stage, Gill was not completely under his respected mentor's influence, an extremely rare phenomenon, for most of Johnston's pupils continued in their master's manner. His personality, philosophy, methods of teaching and enthralling demonstrations on the lecture-room blackboard were apt to turn pupils into disciples. Lacking their master's toughness and charm, they were inclined to escape into the cosy world of calligraphy and the cultivation of an arty-crafty distaste for contemporary life and mass-produced letter-forms. Such distaste was intensified by the fact that lettering and type designs are reproduced by some of the most complex mechanisms of the machine-age, symbols of all that the true scribe must most abhor, or, at best, distrust.

'Johnston confined his work almost entirely to penmanship,' Gill wrote in later reminiscences. 'I did hardly anything in that line and carried his teaching on into lettering in stone, so that it has perhaps unfortunately seemed to many that anything in the way of lettering in stone, which looked like deriving from the revival instigated by Johnston, must be something to do with me, and I daresay I did have some influence in that direction and that there would be some degree of truth in the contention that if I had not done something to improve inscriptions, a lot of the inscribed work of today would be worse than it is, but if you prefer you can put it all down to Edward Johnston.'

As usual, Gill was being mock-modest about his own influence, but it is clear that he saw, in retrospect, that it was his stone-cutting, and, to a lesser degree, his wood-engraving experience that ultimately established his authority as a master of lettering in his own right.

He received his first stone-cutting commission from George Carter, and, from that time on, continued to regard himself as a monumental mason and letter-cutter. He was twenty when he left the architect's office in 1902, confessing later that he wrote to the boss saying he was sorry to leave in what must seem a most improper manner.

Yet he had clearly made his mark on the office, for he received his articles and the promise of any inscriptional work that might be required. He was proud of his claim to be 'a workman' and,

*In a letter to *The Sunday Times* (15.2.1953) following a note on Gill's Pilgrim type by the writer.

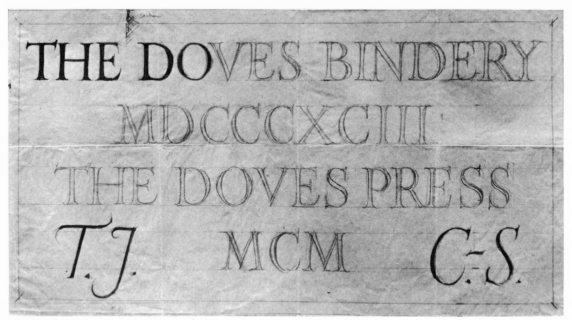

Typical instructional sheet drawn by Gill for a memorial inscription

on his marriage two years later to Ethel Mary Moore, daughter of the beadle of Chichester Cathedral, went to live, almost militantly, in a block of workers' flats, Battersea Bridge Buildings.*

For five years he concentrated on letter-cutting in stone. In a modest way he prospered. He was occasionally short of money but never on the breadline and was invariably able to record solvency in his annual self-accountancy.

These years form one of the more exuberant periods of Gill's crowded life. He was happy in his work and in his marriage, despite one desperate emotional flutter, and he was making more money than he had expected to make in his new career. His gaiety of spirit is evident in those of his letters which survive and in the quality of his work.

Increasing commissions led him to move from Battersea to Hammersmith. He also engaged an assistant, a boy of fifteen, Joseph Cribb, who was about to leave school. This apprenticeship was

---

*Gesture and tenure were resilient. Two years later he moved to Hammersmith, and later rented a studio in Chelsea before going to Ditchling in 1907.

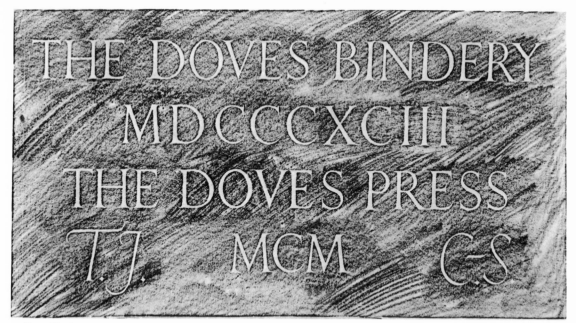

Rubbing of finished inscription

arranged by Emery (later Sir Emery) Walker with whom Cribb's father, a cartographer, was then working. 'When I first went to Gill', Cribb wrote after Gill's death,* 'he had just started on his own in Hammersmith Terrace. Many of the letter-forms he used at that time he discarded later. As his interest in painting and the use and study of type increased, I think he lost interest in the chiselled letter. Yet some of his best inscriptions are his earlier ones. They are freer and have more feeling of the written letter rather than the printed letter.'

Joseph Cribb's younger brother, Laurence, who also became assistant to Gill, added: 'In designing a wall tablet or memorial or even a grave stone, Mr Gill always, as far as possible, put the lettering first and, as it were, built the tablet, etc., around the lettering and not, as is usually done, by designing the panel first and the lettering last, as if the lettering were an afterthought. I think possibly that is why so many of Mr Gill's memorials are so beautiful. He had such great freedom he could do just what he liked with the chisel and the letter. I don't think many of us

* In a letter to the writer.

IN MEMORY OF
SIR HARRY JOHNSTON
G.C.M.G., K.C.B., D.Sc.
ADMINISTRATOR, SOLDIER
EXPLORER, NATURALIST
AUTHOR AND PAINTER
1858 –1927
Vir fortis, audax, mitis, ingenio magno.

Inscription, 1927

pupils got near his great skill. One beautiful example of his own cutting is to be seen in Westminster Abbey: the memorial tablet of the late Sir Frederick Bridges. The first six or seven years I was with Mr Gill, he used to draw the lettering out on the actual stone for me to cut the letters, but after this period I used to draw the lettering out as well as cutting them, although of course, he used to check the work very carefully. Mr Gill made a great master and a perfect teacher. He never seemed to get angry or worried if we made any mistake or even worse broke a stone or two. He used to put great trust in us!'

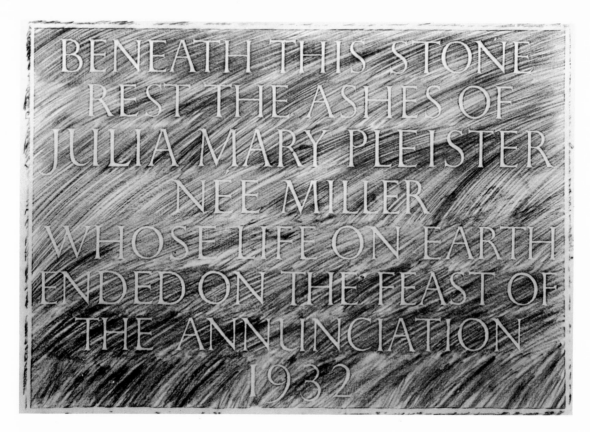

Rubbing of inscription, 1932

Although he had set out on a career as a letter-cutter, Gill was soon involved in many other forms of lettering. Architects were quick to appreciate and patronize a craftsman who understood their requirements. He saved them time, energy and money by relieving them of the necessity for making scale drawings for 'trade' letter-cutters, and he soon had as much of this kind of work as he could handle. He also enlarged his range so that within five years he had not only cut a great number of inscriptions, tombstones and commemorative plaques, but had painted lettering on many shop-fronts (including W. H. Smith's in the rue de Rivoli in Paris in 1903). In 1906 he drew examples of lettering for plates in Johnston's *Writing, Illuminating and Lettering*, and, in 1909 five out of the sixteen plates in Johnston's working supplement to that volume, *Manuscript and Inscription Letters*. Plaster casts of lettering for letter-cutters and sculptors were also made from these plates by Gill and marketed at six shillings each (delivered free in London) by John Hogg of Paternoster Row, publisher of the two books. At the same time Gill made his first attempt at a technical exposition of letter-cutting, which reads somewhat naïvely now. He also engraved, from Johnston's original drawings, headpieces and initial letters for Cobden-Sanderson's Doves Press, and made many drawings and engravings for initial letters and title-pieces for Count Kessler's Cranach Press. Above all, he had also begun those experiments in carving which led to his greater fame.

In almost all the initial letters and titles Gill designed and engraved for Count Kessler between 1905 and 1909, the Johnston influence is emphatic, the calligraphic note marked. Serifs may derive from the graver but the pen is not far distant.

Johnston was still teaching and demonstrating, but, as both instructor and craftsman, he confined himself mainly to chalk and blackboard, reed pen and paper. Gill was gradually forced by his commercial commitments, energy and craftsmanship to examine the possibilities of other materials and other tools, and it was through boxwood and graver, stone and chisel that he escaped from the calligraphic manner.

Of Gill's lettering at that time, a number of examples survive, mostly in the Victoria & Albert Prints and Drawings Room. The alphabets which he drew in 1907 indicate certain lines of development on which he was working, and hand-written notes, accompanying the alphabets, elaborate the points he wished his letter-forms to make. But alphabets and notes still owed much to the immense research upon which Johnston had been occupied for many years. Severance from the Johnston spell was a slow business. Gill's engraved initials for the publications of the St Dominic's Press, for example, published at Ditchling in the years before the First War, are still decoratively Johnstonian in manner. Only in a number of commissions for book-plates for patrons and friends did Gill indicate the beginning of a less formal approach to lettering. Many of the characters he engraved for these small *Ex Libris* labels have a carefree charm not seen elsewhere in his work. Yet they are clearly indicative of his future attitude, their gaiety and movement are far removed from the magisterial formality of Johnston's work, even when the maestro was engaging in one of his more cursive virtuoso displays.

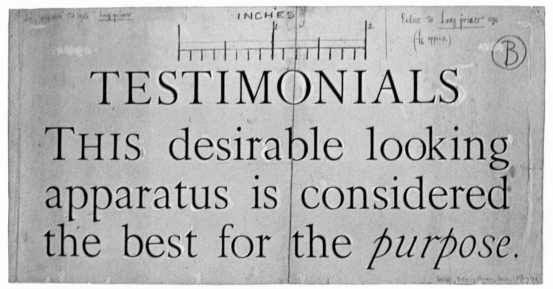

Gill's experiment with enlargement (sixteen times) of Old Style Long Primer

One of the clearest indications of Gill's preoccupation with the notion of evolving a new and more disciplined alphabet is an unusual drawing made by him at Ditchling in 1914. Over a setting in *Old Style Long Primer*, enlarged sixteen times, Gill drew his own variations and adaptations to the letter-forms of the type. The resulting characters are strangely free from the Victorian Old Style tradition which dominated English typographical design at that time.

This experiment may well have been prompted by the success of the new Monotype Imprint design, that remarkable precursor of a wholly new approach to type design. The First War was to intervene before the full significance of Imprint in the printing industry would be assessed. We now see clearly that the introduction of this text type in 1914 was one of the most profound influences in twentieth-century typography. Edward Johnston, Gerard Meynell and J. H. Mason were the chief innovators. Gill, a much younger man, was plainly interested in their experiments and the intoxicating noises of fetter-breaking. That would appear to be the explanation for his own drawing, which presents a somewhat austere, even aseptic, appearance when seen against the body of lettering done by Gill up to that time. Yet the drawing is an important pointer to

ABOVE AND OPPOSITE PAGE: *Typical chapter heads from the Golden Cockerel edition of* THE FOUR GOSPELS, 1931

what was to come. Gill was uncertain in his treatment of the serifs of the lower-case 'p', the italic characters are weak, but a conscious striving after a sterner alphabet is evident. He was certainly gripped by the challenge. In a letter to William (later Sir William) Rothenstein, written in the previous year, he had claimed to 'have got the fly-wheel and the safety-valve of letter-cutting' to hearten him, 'when sculpture and the modern world seem equally bloody'.

Gill's life at Ditchling continued until 1924, interrupted only by brief wartime services – four months during 1918 – in the Royal Air Force Mechanical Transport (where he failed a test for drawing a motor-engine!). Strangely enough, despite his Fabian learnings, he had had some pre-war Territorial Army experience in the Queen's Westminster Volunteer Rifle Corps, and even mentions in his letters rifle-practice at Wormwood Scrubs. The V. & A. records include a proof of a comically light-hearted Union Jack engraved for a concert programme for the 1st Battery of the Canadian Field Artillery serving in France. Curious commission, indeed. And four of his brothers served as soldiers. Nevertheless, this martially-minded pacifist, sound in wind and limb, was exempted from active service, firstly until the completion of his carvings for the *Stations of the Cross in Westminster Cathedral*, and, latterly, because of family commitments. Who will

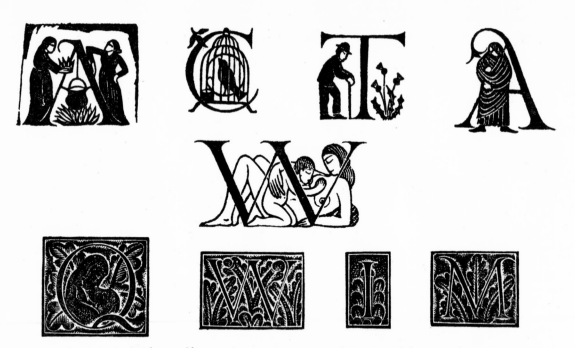

ABOVE AND CENTRE: *Initials engraved for* AUTUMN MIDNIGHT, *poems by Frances Cornford, St Dominic's Press,* 1923

BELOW: *Four initials for the Cranach Press* SONGS OF PRAISE, 1931

say now that British wartime authority is wholly philistine? (Twenty years later Gill was far more of a pacifist and wrote a tract suitable for any conscientious objector's request for exemption from active service.)

Gill's association with Hilary Pepler and the St Dominic's Press was undoubtedly an important factor in arousing his interest in the wider aspects of printing and typography, an association which proved invaluable later and prepared him for an easy partnership with Robert Gibbings and the Golden Cockerel Press and with Stanley Morison of the Monotype Corporation.

In 1924, after a traumatic break with Pepler, Gill and his growing family moved from Ditchling to Capel-y-ffin in South Wales. He was still concerned with letter-cutting, but less as a cutter than as a designer of lettering and supervisor of his assistant's cutting. (His only assistant was Laurence Cribb, Joseph Cribb leaving to start on his own.)

Typical initials engraved for the Golden Cockerel Press

Their main commissions were modest tombstones. Laurence Cribb, writing of a typical task at Capel-y-ffin, says: 'I remember we had two specimen alphabets to do for the South Kensington Museum. I made the panels and he drew the lettering out and told me to cut them. One was incised lettering and the other raised lettering and this sort of lettering I had not done before. I was very worried about it all, but the result seemed to be all right for they are still used, I believe, at most art schools. Mr Gill must have known, however, that it would be all right, but I certainly didn't. I only mention this to show how he trusted us and how he knew more than we did what we could do.' Scores of these directional drawings by Gill and rubbings of the finished results are now in St Bride's Printing Library.

For Gill, his association with Robert Gibbings, dating from 1925 and the publication of *Sonnets and Verses* by Gill's sister, Enid Clay, was especially fortunate. After the somewhat tentative, even

Inscription on hoptonwood stone, 1 9 2 0

shaky early efforts of his first fraternal contribution, he was encouraged by Gibbings to engrave some of the most exuberantly beautiful initials and headings since the time of the monastic scribes, and he was commissioned to design, first, a series of restrained decorative letter-forms for use as initial letters in chapter openings, and, second, a text type for the exclusive use of the Press. This latter commission dovetailed into his work in connection with the design of *Perpetua* for the Monotype Corporation, and the interdependence of the two types is clear to see, especially in the *Perpetua Light Titling*.

ABCDEFG
HIKLMN
OPRSTUV
WXYZJQ

Golden Cockerel Press initials, 1928

ABCDEFGHIJKLMNO
PQURSTVWXYZ

Two-line 18-point initials designed by Eric Gill for the use of the Golden Cockerel Press

GOLDEN COCKEREL
THIRTY-SIX & TWENTY-FOUR
point titling above, and these lines are set in 18 point roman. The type was first used for 'The Four Gospels' in 1931 and is now on loan from Thomas Yoseloff Limited to Will and Sebastian Carter at the Rampant Lions Press, Cambridge, where these lines have been set. ❁ There is a very battered 14 point also, not really worth using, but there is no italic.

Specimen of the Golden Cockerel Press type

The initials were made as wood engravings proper, cut with the graver, although some of his initials were not, strictly speaking, engraved but cut on the side grain or 'plank' of the wood. His zest for experiment never dulled. His initials for the Cranach Press edition of Virgil's *Eclogues and Georgics*, published in 1926, were engraved in this manner to conform with the technique used by Aristide Maillol for the book's decorations. In 1931 he made a series of engravings, mostly nudes, for the Cranach Press edition of *The Song of Solomon*, and a number of initials which seem tentative and fussy when compared with those he was engraving for the Golden Cockerel Press around the same time.

Christopher Sandford, who took over the Golden Cockerel Press from Gibbings, writing of this period in Gill's career, says: 'He spent a chunk of his life – at its most fruitful period – in evolving and perfecting the type of illustrative initial which developed through the four volumes of *The Canterbury Tales* and reached its zenith in *The Four Gospels*. These initials were uniquely Gill and original creative art. Nothing quite like them had ever been done before – nor since – and they are wholly successful. All his study of lettering, of engraving, and of illustration led up to this. In *The Four Gospels* it found its expression.'

Christopher Sandford's claims are well substantiated as anyone fortunate enough to be able to examine *The Four Gospels* can readily confirm. Yet the initials, exuberant, decorative, ornate, seem to run counter to much that Gill had written – and was to write – on the subject of lettering. 'What is good lettering?' he asks in his usual rhetorical fashion at one point in his *Autobiography*, and, as usual, has his answer pat, assuring the reader that he is no teetotaller about fancy work, but that it must be kept subordinate . . . 'and even fancy work', he adds, 'should grow out of legitimate occasion. What is decoration but that which is seemly and appropriate.' Certainly he found an appropriate occasion in *The Four Gospels*.

In 1928, Gill and his family moved from Capel-y-ffin with unconcealed relief. They took over a complex of farm-buildings at Pigotts, high on the hills above High Wycombe in Buckingham-shire. Here Gill was to make his home for the last twelve years of his life.

3

THE TYPE DESIGNS

The Golden Cockerel Press decorative initials are beautiful, but it was his work on the Golden Cockerel Press type which undoubtedly led Gill to design what is perhaps the most majestic of all Roman alphabets for contemporary use. He once said that part of the fascination that lettering held for him was that in this activity, at least, he was concerned only with a thing in itself, and not with its likeness to anything else on earth. 'He was concerned', Denis Tegetmeier has said, 'only to unearth, so to speak, what constitutes the A-ness of the A, the B-ness of the B and so, for us here and now.'

abcdefghijklmn
opqrstuvwxyz &
1234567890

The two alphabets for the Golden Cockerel Press presented no conflict to Gill. His unusually wide experience enabled him to design, with equal assurance, the agreeably flamboyant initials and the more disciplined letter-forms necessary for text. By the time he came to evolve type designs for mass-production any subtle urge to indulge his love of decorative letter-forms was readily subdued.

The Golden Cockerel Press alphabet was required for use as initial letters or in chapter headings to accompany Caslon Old Face as a text type. Only the R (normally one of Gill's most successful letter-forms in any alphabet) has any touch of over-exuberance, and is indeed, for that reason, perhaps the weakest unit in the alphabet. These initials have few affinities with the designs which Gill prepared later for the Monotype *Perpetua Titling*. Perhaps the letter-forms G H L I M U V Z, but no others.

That Gill was becoming master of the strange technological processes required in this new craft is decisively shown in his designs for the Golden Cockerel Press type – not to be confused with the

ABCDEFGHI JKLMNOPQR STUVW&XYZ

Gill's preliminary designs for the Felicity type, 1926

initials – first used in A. E. Coppard's *Hundredth Story**. To typographical students, this type, both in its titling and its italic, is closely linked with the later *Perpetua* roman and the *Felicity* and *Joanna* italics or 'sloped romans'. Undoubtedly Gill owed as much to Gibbings in this earlier phase of his type-designing career as, later, he did to Stanley Morison.

Certain developments in Gill's alphabets up to this time are clearly evident. In 1907, for instance, he was frequently using a straight, downward stroke to the upper-case R, to be seen in several of his wood engravings. By 1909 his stone-cutting had produced a curved stroke, which is exaggerated in the engraved Golden Cockerel Press type. In this latter design it is the most distinctive character in the alphabet, far less subtle than the same character in *Perpetua*. Again, the

---

*The goodwill, stocks and types of the Golden Cockerel Press were sold in 1959 by Christopher Sandford to the New York publishers, Thomas Yoseloff Ltd. The latter firm published two books using the types but then seem to have decided that such esoteric ventures were not for them, and made the Golden Cockerel Press type available for sale.

Meantime, the type has been loaned to the Rampant Lions Press of Cambridge (see specimen p.30) where the 36, 24, 18 and a somewhat woebegone 14 point have been used in a single-sheet limited edition keepsake issued by the Press. Unfortunately, the italic version of the type seems to have vanished.

ABCDEFG HIJKLMN OPQRSTU VWXYZ

lower-case g, in the roman and italic alphabets of 1909, are the forms which he successfully continued in almost all his type designs, including Perpetua, and even the famous sans serif design.

The lower-case roman and italic r is another letter-form which should be compared in its evolving stages. In the 1907 alphabet the cross-stroke to the lower-case r was too emphatic. In the chiselled 1909 alphabet some attempt has been made to discipline the form. With the design of Golden Cockerel Press type and Perpetua between 1925 and 1930 the r has been resolved and made into a cooperative member of the alphabet.

A MOVABLE TYPE IS THE

A B C D E F G
H I J K L M N
O P Q R S T U
V W X Y Z

ABCDEFGHIJKLMNO
PQRSTUVWXYZ
abcdefghijklmnopqrst
uvwxyz

The Johnston Underground sans serif

A comparison of sans serifs

The three types shown on this and the opposite page are representative of the three stages in the development of the sans serif form between the two wars. Edward Johnston's design, a breakaway from the nineteenth-century grotesques, was clean-cut but affected by one or two intrusive mannerisms, particularly the lower-case l, and the diamond-shaped dots over i and j were odd, to say the least.

Paul Renner's Futura was the most extreme example of the Germanic Compasses-and-Set-Square School, and the various weights of this type were popular in this country, along with the Erbar series, designed by Joseph Erbar, until the Monotype Corporation introduced the Gill Sans Serif in 1927. The natural development of Gill's design from traditional models (together with the possibilities of its widespread use on the Monotype machine) gained a considerable European and later American reputation for the type.

By 1925, at the request of Stanley Morison, typographical adviser to the Monotype Corporation, Gill was ready to start on his drawings for a new alphabet for that organisation. This design was to become known as *Perpetua*. In that year he was also engaged upon another alphabetical project of considerable interest to himself. In May 1925, writing to Desmond Chute, his most intimate friend, an ex-Slade student who later became a priest, he says: 'I'm doing a set of alphabets for the Army & Navy Stores – for them to use for all their notices and signs! This is an interesting job – for it is: how to do, 1, good letters, 2, absolutely legible-to-the-last-degree letters, 3, letters which any fool can copy accurately and easily. So I'm doing them simple block letters. It's rather

36

ABCDEFGHIJKLMNOP
QRSTUVWXYZ
abcdefghijklmnopqrstu
vwxyz

Futura Medium, 48 pt

ABCDEFGHIJKLMN
OPQRSTUVWXYZ
abcdefghijklmnopqrs
tuvwxyz

Monotype Gill Sans Medium Series 262, 48 pt

abcdefg

pqr

Before and after

Although the Gill Sans Serif design is now wholly attributed to Gill, it should be mentioned and remembered that, like most other latter-day type designers, Eric Gill owed a great deal to his mechanical advisers and helpers. The two sets of letter-forms compared on these two pages show part of the debt which Gill owed to such advice. Perhaps the most noteworthy changes during the transition of the letter-forms from drawing-board to matrices, were the adjustments (suggested and made by the Monotype punch-cutters) to Gill's original notion for slanting cut-offs to

fun cutting out great big letters out of white paper and sticking them on big black sheets – they don't half stare at you – fine test for astigmatism.' Unfortunately, no trace of this alphabet or his Beggarstaff-Brothers-type experiments remains. Or for another alphabet, which, John Dreyfus believes, was projected for the Cunard shipping line.

The first of the many Gill Sans Serif variants in size, weight and nomenclature was shown by the Monotype Corporation in 1929, and thus ante-dated the first showing of Perpetua, although Gill dated the latter type as 1925, and the sans as from 1927 onwards.

abcdefg

the ascenders and descenders of the b d p q characters. By making right-angled cut-offs to these characters the Monotype mechanics made an important contribution to the manifold virtues of the design.

Even more important was the attention given to the lower-case g. No other character in the roman alphabet gives so many headaches to the letter designer. Gill liked a fair degree of freedom for the lower bowl to his lower-case g, probably a legacy from his stone-cutting days. This freedom was curtailed in a masterly and entirely satisfactory manner, both mechanically and aesthetically, by the Monotype technicians. These variants are reproduced from the original trial drawings.

pqr

Gill Sans was an English contribution and/or answer to that spate of sans serifs which flooded from the German type foundries after the remarkable success of Paul Renner's Futura design* which had been introduced by the Bauer Typefoundry of Frankfurt-on-Main in 1927.

---

* Josef Erbar had been commissioned by Ludwig and Mayer as early as 1913 to design a 'precise, mechanically-produced reading type in the sans serif form', but Renner's design was quickly established in Germany as the 'true' sans serif, the logical typographical innovation for a machine-run age. And as the logical expression of a true sans serif form it stands alone, although the later Univers series is a close rival.

ABOVE AND OPPOSITE: *Drawings made by Gill in 1928 for the poster version of his sans serif type for the London & North-Eastern Railway*

Gill's Monotype sans serif has many of those features which were soon to become recognisable Gill characteristics. The type certainly derives in part from the sans serif type which Johnston had designed for the use of the London Underground in 1916. This is understandable, for both Gill and Gerard Meynell were present at the first conference at which Frank Pick, head of London Underground publicity, and Johnston discussed the sans serif which the latter was to design for the organization. Yet the derivation is not emphatic, and, as we have seen, although Gill thought there was little to choose between the two types, he plainly thought he owed little to Johnston in his own design. And he had been experimenting on his own account for he showed a 'block

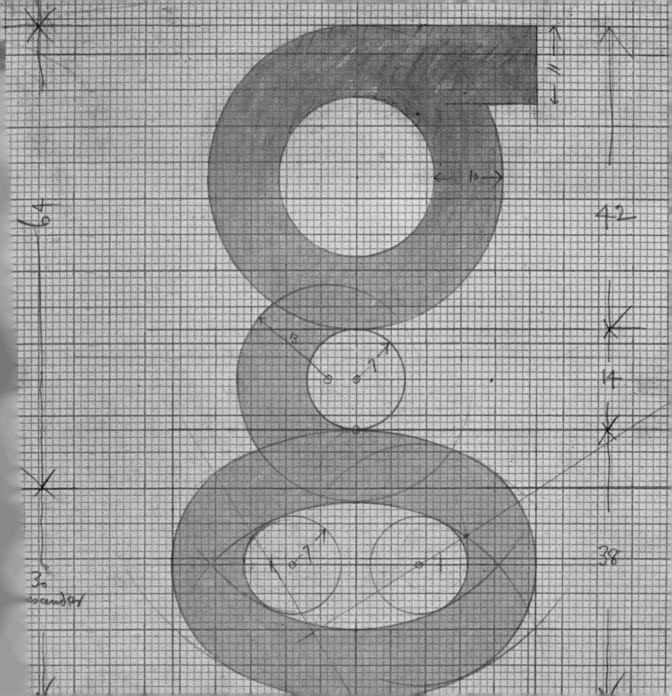

64

42

13

14

10

38

30
esander

ABCDEFG

HIJKLMN

OPQRSTY

UVWXZ&

LEFT: *Gill's first experimental drawings (reduced) for the upper-case italic version of his sans serif design*

ABOVE: *Gill's initial drawings (reduced) for the lower-case italic version of the sans serif design*

letter' with almost imperceptible serifs in his revision of G. S. Welch's *Ship Painter's Manual*, published in the same year.

On the other hand he did owe a great deal to others. Although *Gill Sans* is nominally attributed to Gill (and according to legend, derived from a fascia board he had designed for Douglas Cleverdon's bookshop in Bristol), he owed, in company with all other modern type designers, a considerable debt to his technical advisers and collaborators, particularly to those in the drawing-office and, above all, to the punch-cutters. A comparison of Gill's original designs with the revisions made by the Monotype technicians gives some indication of the help that Gill received. As originally projected, Gill's sans serif would certainly not have held its own in company with either *Futura* or *Erbar*. Or, for that matter, with Johnston's. But he had the wit to learn quickly from those who could advise him in this new technology, and in its final form *Gill Sans* proved superior to all others available to printers and typographers who might be interested in having a sans serif type that was not a dehumanized, wholly mechanistic alphabet.

In a sense, of course, all the post-war sans serifs derived from Johnston's teaching and influence, but a comparison of designs by Johnston, Erbar, Renner and Gill shows that Gill's is the most reasonable and readable of these letter-forms, set far apart from the T-square precision of the German types and the occasional fussiness of Johnston's alphabet. Gill's sans serif eschewed those qualities of ornament and decoration implicit in serif construction, but retained enough colour and relief in the distribution of weight throughout each character and throughout the fount, to save the type from that wearing monotony normally inseparable from sans serif settings of any length. Gill's is the most readable and legible (not always synonymous qualities) of all the modern sans serif designs, yet even his design has severe limitations as a text type, limitations which are unfortunately not always regarded, and were not always so regarded by Gill in his own printing-shop. The ultimate unreadability of even this, the most civilized of sans serifs, may be seen from a study of quite a brief text set in *Gill Sans*.

This is the 12-point size of the Monotype *Gill Sans Serif* in its medium weight. Despite its adherence to the traditional shapes of the roman alphabet, the type has the defects of all sans serif types for textual work. The absence of serifs gives a vertical emphasis throughout settings of any length, whereas our eyes, from earliest reading days, have been accustomed to that logical horizontal stress imposed by serif construction. Typo-graphical revolutionaries might contend that this is merely slavish acceptance of convention, but most eyes, after trials of sans serif and serif text types, are likely to agree with convention.

In the 10-point size the demerits of the sans serif form are even more apparent. Even in timetables and other tabular settings, serifs have been found to have considerable value.

Finally, this is the 8-point size, which is useful for limited tabulated details and footnotes, but never for text settings.

No other sans serif type would stand up to even that modest demonstration.

ABCDEFGHIJKLMNO
PQRSTUVWXYZabcde
fghijklmnopqrstuvwxyz
ABDEGHJKMNQRS
TUVWXYZabcdefgh
ijklmnopqrstuvwxyz

A comparison of the structural similarities between Perpetua and Gill Sans in 48 pt

The qualities which give *Gill Sans* its admittedly limited usefulness as a text type are mainly those which link this type with *Perpetua*. A comparison of the 48-point sizes of the *Gill Sans* and *Perpetua* clearly shows their pronounced similarities of structure, both deriving from his long and intensive training as a letter-cutter. Those similarities of structure disappear with a vengeance in the display variants which were later based on the *Gill Sans* prototype. Shadow letters and block-busting heavyweights were built on to and around the austere prototype.

Although the master letter-cutter affected to despise the riproaring fairground and market-place pleasures of display typography, he joined in the free-for-all in a genially two-faced

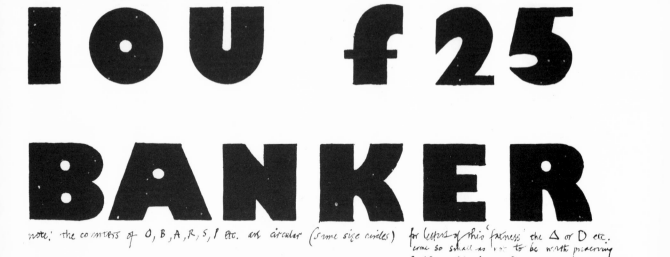

Gill's drawings for the most weighty of the variants on his sans serif theme : Monotype Gill Sans Ultra Bold, Series 442

manner. He severely castigated such types (in his *Essay on Typography*,* for instance) dismissing them as 'absurd misconceptions', 'sans overbold' and 'unseemly abnormalities and exaggerations' (even documenting his denunciation with examples not dissimilar from the Monotype heavyweights based on *Gill Sans*). Yet he allowed display types such as the *Gill Shadow* (three

*An Essay on Typography. Published by Sheed & Ward, 1931.

ABCDEFGHIKL

Gill Sans Cameo, Monotype Series 233

ABCDEFGHIJKLM

Gill Sans Shadow Line, Monotype Series 290

ABCDEFGHIJKM

Gill Sans Cameo Ruled, Monotype Series 299

ABCDEFGHIJKL

Gill Sans Shadow, Monotype Series 304

ABCDEFGHIJK

Gill Sans Shadow, Monotype Series 406

ABCDEFGHLM

Gill Sans Ultra Bold, Monotype Series 442

variants), *Gill Cameo* and others to carry his name without demur. The designs for *Gill Extra Bold*, the most horrendous and blackguardedly of these display exploitations are, for example, clearly initialled by him and carry his own – no doubt self-deprecating – title: *Double-elefans*. He thus has nominal responsibility for a dozen of the most darksome display types of his time. Not for the first or last time did Gill let his right hand know overmuch about the sometimes dubious, or, at least, devious talents of his left. He wasn't a skilful dialectician for nothing.

So much for what might be accounted for Gill's typographical peccadilloes. He would undoubtedly have claimed that these exploitations were other men's notions and that his own integrity as a lettering artist was still intact. He was certainly nearer to the manner of William Caslon or John Baskerville than any of his type-designing contemporaries. His lifelong preoccupation was the classical Roman alphabet.

Perpetua is undoubtedly the finest classical alphabet evolved in this country between the eras of *Caslon* and *Baskerville* and our own time, with the possible exception of *Bell*. Other notable printing types had been produced between the two World Wars, but these models were, in the main, unashamed revivals of earlier native types, such as *Baskerville*, *Caslon* and *Bell*, and such early continental masterpieces as *Plantin*, *Fournier* and *Garamond*, all elements in that remarkable programme initiated by Stanley Morison and William Burch, Managing Director of the Monotype Corporation at the time. Apart from its other considerable merits, *Perpetua* was distinguished from these types by its originality, which had nothing in common with the self-conscious, self-indulgent oddities of other contemporary would-be classic faces such as *Pastonchi* or some of Frederic Goudy's types. *Perpetua* is clearly a disciplined design that derives from Gill's earlier experience and experiments.

As Morison explained afterwards*, the fine serif in origin is not written but sculptured and in seeking a new type of that order, Gill was the obvious choice and was 'asked to make drawings of the letters he had long been habitually carving'. As the retention of the chiselled quality of Gill's letter-forms was of paramount importance, Morison decided not to have direct photographic and pantographic reproductions of the drawings. Instead they were passed to Charles Malin, the foremost of French type-cutters, and a set of punches of the upper and lower-case in the 12-point (equivalent to the rarely used 13-point size in Anglo-American type usage) Didot size was cut in 1926 and a set of titling capitals in October of the same year. Morison contended that the

*In *A Tally of Types* privately printed for Cambridge University Press, 1953.

48

Aa Bb Cc Dd Ee Ff Gg Hh Ii Jj Kk Ll Mm Nn Oo Pp Qq Rr Ss Tt Uu Vv Ww Xx Yy Zz 1234567890

Perpetua Roman, *Monotype Series 239, 48 pt*

Felicity was the outcome of a number of compromises, but the type seems easily to triumph over these. He added that the titling capitals, i.e. Monotype series 258, 'would be esteemed as long as the Latin alphabet remains the basis of Western recorded civilization. The lower case of the display sizes from 30-point to 72-point is also magnificent, especially the roman. And this is natural, inevitable. The design originated in Gill's inscriptional lettering, not in a book-script, for he had none. Had it been possible for him to be interested enough in calligraphy to transcribe books in the equivalent of 16-point or, better, 12-point, it is abundantly possible that his Perpetua would have realized to the maximum the intentions of its producers.'

Perpetua is never dull and its beauties always rediscoverable. The alphabet is undoubtedly seen in its most majestic form in the 72-point Titling, but is also handsome when upper and lower case are used in some brief injunction or declamatory passage in the 18-point or 14-point size. The firm and authoritative structure of each letter-form is then clearly seen. Such subtleties as the curve of the final downward stroke of the upper-case R; the balanced M; the able grouping of the ungainly components of W; the balance of solid and void in G, are taken care of in masterly fashion. Then consider the lower-case: the involved yet simple a; the masterly arrangement of

49

lmabcdefghijk

t k l n apoqefgr

suvwxyz

Perpetua Italic

Gill's first experimental drawings (reduced) for the italic version of Perpetua, a good deal more sloped than the earlier design for Felicity (see p. 33) the opposed bowls in g (the most wayward letter-form in the English language); the felicitous tail to the y, giving necessary weight to the descender so that it should not intrude into the alphabet by its very lightness; the pleasing curves to m and n. Apart from *Jubilee*, none of Gill's later typographical designs departed radically from the essential structure of the letter-forms in *Perpetua*. The same paradox of decorative austerity is apparent, even in his sans serif design.

By a mischance, the italic, which is now so widely used, is less pleasing than the earlier version, a true sloped roman named *Felicity*, amongst the most agreeably decorative yet readable of all sloped forms. Unfortunately, this exquisite type has been displaced by the more mundane *Perpetua Italic*. A few printing houses have *Felicity*, but even in those, the use of the type is restricted and thus scarcely known. The story of *Felicity* is doubtless no more than a lesser tragedy in one of the lesser studies of mankind, but sad enough all the same.

Experiments relating to *Perpetua*, between 1925 and 1930, undoubtedly influenced Gill's other types. The *Golden Cockerel* type, designed in 1929, is essentially an expanded and rounded version of *Perpetua*, lacking the beauty of the Monotype fount, but readable, sturdy and dignified, peculiarly well adapted for use with wood-engravings.

In the same way that he had given a sense of sanity to the sans serif vogue, Gill attempted to introduce those qualities into the then-current vogue for Egyptian types. Monotype *Solus*, dated 1929, possesses undoubted merits, but it also had two considerable disadvantages: it was produced too late to catch the market in what was an unashamed novelty vogue, and it lacked those aggressive qualities which gave *Beton*, *Memphis*, *Karnak*, and Monotype *Rockwell* their wide popularity amongst advertising typographers and commercial printers. *Solus* is a pleasant enough type, with more than a hint of its *Perpetua* sponsorship, and it is obvious that Gill had devoted considerable attention to the problem of trying to make a slab-serif type design reasonable in design and readable in practice. Yet *Solus* held too delicate a hint of some of the more reticent of nineteenth-century Egyptians for twentieth-century tastes. The serifs were added with subtlety and were not mere slab appendages. In the self-assertive world of publicity such delicacy had no place. In the smaller sizes of *Solus*, the *Perpetua* sponsorship is so obvious that most readers would probably be unaware of differences.

A bold version of *Solus* was also produced, but this type lacked, even more emphatically, the qualities which were at that time deemed necessary in an Egyptian: blackness and insistent slab serifs. Gill tried to retain a semblance of the true Roman letter-form, and almost succeeded in

FGH FGH

to be by Quinctilian. Indeed, they are in perfect accordance
with the whole Platonic system. Bacon's views, as may easily be
supposed, were widely different. The powers of the memory,
he observes, without the help of writing, can do little towards
the advancement of any useful science. He acknowledges that

with the whole Platonic system. Bacon's views, as may easily
be supposed were widely different. The powers of the memory, he observes, without the help of writing, can do little
towards the advancement of any useful science He acknowledges that the memory may be disciplined to such a point as

ABOVE LEFT: From an experimental line-block made for Gill during the Solus discussions between the artist and the Monotype Corporation
RIGHT: From the artist's final drawing for Solus   BELOW: Monotype Solus Series 276 and Solus Bold Series 368

that endeavour, but he certainly failed to design a letter-form with any pronounced appeal for
designers of advertisements.

Gill also dated the *Perpetua Greek* fount for 1929, but these dates were given at a later date and set
arbitrary limits upon what had been a continuous working programme. (Studying Gill's original
drawings it seems fairly clear that from time to time he gave dates to drafts which he plainly
thought more apposite.) Even a designer as energetic as Gill could scarcely have produced three
good designs in one year, and he was never anxious to compete with the prolific output of
Frederic Goudy, the American type-designer, who designed over one hundred types.

According to a note in *The Monotype Recorder**, Gill's objective in designing his *Perpetua Greek* was
not only to harmonize, but as far as possible, to integrate the Roman and Greek alphabets. He
plainly hoped to evolve a basic graeco-roman type, possessed of special characters as required,

*The Monotype Recorder, Vol 41, No. 3, 1958. A special number commemorating an exhibition of Gill's lettering and
type designs which was held at the Monotype Corporation's London HQ.

Οι μεν πολλοι των ενθαδε ηδη ειρηκοτων επαινουσι τον προσθεντα τω νομω τον λογον τονδον επι τοις εκ των πολεμων θαπτομενοις αγορευεσθαι αυτον. εμοι δε αρκουν αν εδοκει ειναι ανδρων αγαθων εργω γενουενων εργω και δηλουσθαι τας τιμας οια και νυν περι τον ταφον τονδε δημοσια παφασκευασθεντα ορατε, και μη εν ενι ανδρι πολλων αρετας κινδυνευεσθαι ευ τε και χειρον ειποντι πιστευθηναι. χαλεπον γαρ το μετριως ειπειν εν ω μολις και η δοκησις της αληθειας βεβαιουται. ο τε γαρ ξυνειδως και ευνους ακροατης ταχ αν τι ενδεεστερως προς α βουλεται τε και επισταται νομισειε δηλουσθαι, ο τε απειρος εστιν α και πλεοναζεσθαι, δια φθονον, ει τι υπερ την αυτου φυσιν ακουοι. μεχρι γαρ τουδε ανεκτοι οι επαιμοι

Monotype Perpetua Greek Series 283

but of common structure wherever possible. 'Accents were to be eliminated as a late accretion from the scholiasts.' (Does one detect the Morison touch here?)

Gill's approach to an alphabet which is traditionally cut 'in italic' resulted in a beautiful, functional and unusually evenly-coloured type design, but the scholiasts had their perhaps inevitable revenge. Although Perpetua Greek is undoubtedly the most aesthetically assured of all Greek types it has found no favour with the compilers of Greek texts and has never had the showing the design deserves.* Classicists still continue with their favoured Porson Greek Series 106, while modernists seem to prefer Times Greek Series 565.

---

*Although the Gill Greek did not meet with the approval of the British academics, the type was appreciated nearer home, as it were, for at the request of a newspaper in Nicosia, Cyprus, Gill Sans Greek, Series 572, was cut by the Monotype Corporation in display sizes around 1953. A year or so later the 6, 8, 10, and 12 point were ordered, and in 1957 the 11 point was cut, together with the Gill Sans Greek Inclined, Series 571. In 1958 the Monotype Corporation also cut a bold and a light version, Series 625 and 672 respectively, for the Greek market, and also cut the Condensed Gill Greek, Series 585, also for newspaper usage in Cyprus.

This is a specimen of 36-point Joanna in the Monotype version Series 478 and this is *Joanna Italic*. It was produced in 1937 from the original drawings made by Eric Gill.

Joanna Roman and Italic, Monotype Series 478

Gill's Joanna, the type in which these words are set, is perhaps the most engaging of all his type designs and was first shown in 1930. The type was designed by Gill for his own printing-shop, which he had established with his son-in-law, Réné Hague, at Pigotts at Hughendon near High Wycombe, in Buckinghamshire, to which he had removed in 1928. That first version of the type was engraved and cut at the Caslon Letter Foundry, now incorporated in the Stephenson Blake type foundry of Sheffield. The Monotype Corporation made their version for machine composition in 1937.

Gill was at pains to establish that Pigotts was not in the English private press tradition. He had no wish to link himself with the preciosities of Cobden-Sanderson, Morris, St John Hornby and the rest of the *rentier* printer-publishers. He was much too earthy for that.

In his usual forceful dialectical manner, he contended* that 'private press' was a difficult term to define, but immediately, of course, plunged into definition.

'The real distinction between such a press and others', he wrote, 'is not in the typographical enthusiasm of its proprietors, but simply in the fact that a "private" press prints solely what it chooses to print, whereas a "public" press prints what its customers demand of it.

*In a letter to The Monotype Recorder, 1933   INSET: Gill's original design for Joanna roman and italic

MWHKTUJXZYN
CGDⅭSⅢBPR¶ÆⅨ
bcdéohijrmpqskgzty

w x & æ œ) f f f ff fi fl ; ?

o g a q b e d h m n i j k p q u h v w

z æ œ & c o e fl r 1 2 3 4 5 6 7 8

'Doubtless the circumstances of a private press enable it to pay more attention to questions of typography aesthetic and otherwise, while the public printer is very often at the mercy of his customers, especially in these days wherein the press is run more as a purely business affair, that is to say an affair having only financial success as a test.

'On the other hand it is obvious that private presses suffer from their very freedom, and in many cases have been conspicuous for the worst kind of self-conscious artistic eccentricity, while the public press in spite of its financial obsession – the tyranny of auditors and share-holders – often achieve a good reasonable commonplace and therefore pleasant standard of excellence.

'It remains clear that much useful experimental work has been done by the private presses and that many business houses have not failed to take advantage of the fact.

'I think it would be good if we could all agree that the distinction between private and public is what the words themselves suggest, and has nothing whatever to do with the use of machinery, whether hand-driven or otherwise, or with questions of the artistic quality of the product.'

Few would dispute these views so long as the result, in either case, were to prove as pleasant as the *Joanna* and *Joanna Italic*.

Joanna Italic is, without doubt, Gill's most successful version of the sloped roman. For some typographers, this type remains the most individual and successful of all Gill's type designs. The letter-forms have character and beauty, discipline and gaiety. No other alphabet of this century has managed to make typographical affectation so readable. We would have to go back to the *Fell* types to find a type so wayward in design and yet so easy on the eye.

In his two earlier solutions to the problem of designing an italic to accompany successful roman type designs, Gill was less traditional than was his habit. He had obviously marked, learned and digested Stanley Morison's notes concerning the requirements for a 'sloped roman' rather than the more pronounced slope of the conventional italic form.

Joanna also exemplified another of Gill's theories. He had long doubted the necessity for the pronounced emphasis between the thick and thin strokes of the roman alphabet which had been practised by stone-cutters and other makers of alphabets since Roman times.

The classical incised letter-form, progenitor of all Western lettering, had its own tradition of thick and thin stroke, the origins of which are obscure. The thick and thin strokes in calligraphy

H O W oft when thou my musike musike playst,

Upon that blessed wood whose motion sounds

With thy sweet fingers when thou gently swayst,

The wiry concord that mine eare confounds,

Do I envie those Jackes that nimble leape,

To kisse the tender inward of thy hand,

Whilst my poore lips which should that harvest reape,

At the woods bouldness by thee blushing stand.

To be so tikled they would change their state,

And situation with those dancing chips,

Ore whome thy fingers walke with gentle gate,

Making dead wood more blest then living lips,

Since sausie Jackes so happy are in this,

Give them thy fingers, me thy lips to kisse.

T H ' E X P E N C E of Spirit in a waste of shame

Is lust in action, and till action, lust

Is perjurd, murdrous, blouddy, full of blame,

Savage, extreame, rude, cruell, not to trust,

Injoyd no sooner but dispised straight,

Past reason hunted, and no sooner had

Past reason hated as a swollowed bayt,

On purpose layd to make the taker mad.

Madde in pursuit and in possession so,

Had, having, and in quest to have, extreame,

A blisse in proofe and provd a very wo,

Before a joy proposd behind a dreame,

All this the world well knowes yet none knowes well,

To shun the heaven that leads men to this hell.

Double-page opening from S H A K E S P E A R E ' S S O N N E T S set in Joanna Italic (Cassell 1933)

are determined by the width of the pen, the angle at which the pen is held and the direction in which it is directed. Gill taught his pupils, especially latterly, to reduce the emphasis between thick and thin to a minimum. What Gill learned in the disciplines of chisel and stone he was apt to impart to alphabetical experiments in other media.

THIS is a specimen of the *Aries* type designed by Eric Gill in 18 point, 14 point and 10 point roman and *italic* for Fairfax Hall at The Stourton Press. The cost of design, punches and matrices was paid by Sir Percival David on condition that the types were used for the first time in the catalogue of his pottery and porcelain which R. L. Hobson, C.B. was preparing between 1930 and 1934. (*That was 18 point. This is 14 point italic, followed by a sentence in roman and the final sentence is in 10 point.*) Since that time The Stourton Press has published a small number of limited editions, mostly in *Aries* and some not for sale. All but two published last year are out of print.

The Aries type (Stourton Press)

In this view he was certainly consistent. Twenty years previously he had enjoined Desmond Chute and Albert Cribb to 'keep the thin strokes nice and thin and the thick strokes not too fat', adding, for, good measure, 'you can have quite modern lettering with no difference of thick and thin at all'.

In the *Joanna Italic*, each character, judged individually, is affected and should thus intrude into the fount. The *c* and *e* are most casually curved; the *a* is too like the *o*; the *w* is too wide for the set of the rest of the alphabet; the downstroke of the *y* is too sharp; the *g* seizes too swiftly upon the eye. These are just criticisms. Yet, like so many triumphs of seemingly casual artistry, the type in composition has an evenness of colour which defies the laws of optics and the dicta of pundits. Here is none of the mannered affectations of, say, *Pastonchi* or *Locarno*, which are quickly wearying to the eye. In *Joanna*, a master of letter-forms engaged upon a pleasurable task for his own delight. Here too, he was consistent, for many of the *Joanna* characters echo the innocent gaiety of those engraved for the book-plates he had designed twenty years earlier.

Few types designed for a private press have been subject to so little querying from an exigent patron aware of what he likes. *Joanna Italic* (for which only a lower-case was designed, as Gill used his roman capitals in accordance with notable precedents) is defiant of almost every typographical canon of the day, except perhaps Morison's authoritative directive towards the sloped roman as the ideal italic form. *Joanna Italic* is gaily triumphant. The only demerit of the type, according to its several enthusiasts, is its present obscurity, for too few printers own the type.

Gill dated the design of *Aries*, which he designed for the Stourton Press, as 1932, although the type was not seen in a printed page until 1934. This type was also cut and cast by the Caslon Letter Foundry, although all subsequent casting was done by Fairfax Hall, founder of the Stourton Press, using a pivotal type-caster. *Aries* is a sober design. Certain characteristics suggest that Gill may have been influenced by a sight of trial cuttings of *Times New Roman*, which was then in production, preparatory to its first use in *The Times* of October 3rd, 1932. Several of the lower-case letter-forms would seem to derive from Morison's experiments with the traditional *Caslon* alphabet (a, e, d, h, m, n). The sobriety of the type is in startling contrast with the near-fabulous nature of its commission and use, for *Aries* was designed for use in one book: *A Catalogue of Chinese Pottery and Porcelain.** An element in the commission was that the type should be suitable for use in a page containing Chinese types or reproductions of Chinese vase inscriptions, and Gill consulted many specimens of Chinese calligraphy whilst making drawings. In the opinion of Fairfax Hall, the design 'helped to give unity to what might have been a typographer's nightmare', and with that opinion few are likely to disagree. In a wider market, *Aries* might well have

---

*The book deserves a special note on its own account. *A Catalogue of Chinese Pottery and Porcelain in the Collection of Sir Percival David, Bt*, to give its title in full, was published by the Stourton Press, London, in 1934, in an edition of 650 copies. The book contained 180 plates, most of them printed in colour, some in six and seven workings. Each plate was printed separately, usually with the specimen of pottery placed before the printer so that every subtlety of colour should, if possible, be reproduced. The plates were printed on specially made super-calendered paper; on one side of the sheet, each pair of plates being bound in with a double fold; blank versos were thus avoided. The text was printed on hand-made paper with friezes of a border design and a repeat motif of celestial rams in white at the head.

Fairfax Hall later used the *Aries* type in other books published by his Stourton Press, notably in Marlowe's *Hero and Leander* (1935) and in *The Strange Life of Ivan Osokin* (1949).

In 1949 Fairfax Hall moved to South Africa where he set up the Stourton Press afresh and printed and published a number of books under the imprint. He returned to London in 1961 and set up his Press once again, this time in Kensington. That the Stourton Press had not lost its unique supremacy amongst modern private presses was shown in the first book, published after his return. *Paintings and drawings by Harold Gilman and Charles Ginner in the Collection of Edward Le Bas*, which took three years to print and was published in 1965, and in which the colour plates were reproduced with a verisimilitude unsurpassed by any commercial house in Europe.

ABCDEFGH
IKLMNOPR
STUWXYabcde
fghijklmnopqrstuwxy

Jubilee (Stephenson Blake) 72 pt, 60 pt and 48 pt sizes

proved a useful type in the Times Roman manner, offering a slightly richer printing surface on
calendered paper than its famous prototype. The type, however, has been retained for the
exclusive use of the Stourton Press.

During 1933 and 1934 Gill was at work on drawings and revisions of two types, Jubilee and
Bunyan. Jubilee, commissioned by Stephenson Blake of Sheffield, is a display type which suggests
that Gill was wise to step aside from any temptation to design alphabets for advertisers, for
the type is not especially successful as an attempt to invest the traditional alphabet with those
uncial characteristics which Victor Hammer and other designers had given to certain German
types. The design was hurriedly produced to coincide with a regal celebration, and this may
account for some of its less successful features, particularly the angled cut-offs of ascenders and

Through France & Italy

have perished ere he could have ask'd one for himself: he stood by the chaise, a little without the circle, and wiped a tear from a face which I thought had seen better days—Good God! said I—and I have not one single sous left to give him—But you have a thousand! cried all the powers of nature, stirring within me—so I gave him—no matter what—I am ashamed to say how much, now—and was ashamed to think how little, then; so if the reader can form any conjecture of my disposition, as these two fixed points are given him, he may judge within a livre or two what was the precise sum.

I could afford nothing for the rest, but 'Dieu vous benisse'—Et le bon Dieu vous benisse encore—said the old soldier, the dwarf, &c. The pauvre honteux could say nothing—he pull'd out a little handkerchief, and wiped his face as he turned away—and I thought he thanked me more than them all.

Specimen of the Bunyan type with Perpetua Italic chapter heading from Laurence Sterne's A SENTIMENTAL JOURNEY

descenders, the half-serifs and the lower-case g, x, w and y. In notes which Gill wrote for the type founders, he claimed that the ordinary 'black letter' had its uses, but that it was too angular and illegible for modern eyes. He contended that there was a place for a type which derived its forms from the pen but retained the roundness, openness and legibility of the traditional roman faces. Jubilee was his attempt to design such a type. 'The character of its thick and thin', he wrote, 'is derived from pen writing as also is the character of the graduations from thick to thin. The O, for example, is not an oval in a circle but two circles overlapping. It is a heavy letter and at the same time an open one. In deference to demand an alphabet of capitals has been designed to "go" with it: but there is not properly a capital alphabet for this type of letter and it would be better to follow the ancient practice of using roman capitals for initials.' It is doubtful whether many advertising typographers would have been keen to act on that suggestion.

Bunyan may be considered as a careful balance between the *Golden Cockerel* type and *Joanna*. The type was engraved and cast at the Caslon Letter Foundry for Gill's exclusive use at Pigotts. Only a roman version, which is seen in a specimen page above, taken from *A Sentimental Journey** was designed, although a few trial drawings were made for a proposed sloped roman.

Bunyan is a rounded and pleasing type, its colour evenly disposed. No letter-form, with the possible exception of the lower-case g, is intrusive or ill-balanced in text settings. *Bunyan* later became more widely known, for in 1950, the Linotype organization purchased from Gill's widow, the rights to produce the *Bunyan* design. Punches, patterns and drawings were taken over from Réné Hague, and large-scale drawings made from the punches. The few tentative drawings of an italic version of the type formed the basis of the italic accompaniment to the Linotype version of *Bunyan*, which was renamed *Pilgrim*.

The family likeness between *Perpetua*, *Solus*, *Joanna* and the *Pilgrim* roman alphabets is clear. The differences are subtleties, and it was in the sensitive and judicious control of such subtleties that Gill showed his true skill as a maker of alphabets, for it is far easier to design an altogether novel A than to refine the authority of the Trajan initial. And in his willingness to concentrate upon this continuous refinement Gill was alone amongst the type-designers of his time.

Amongst Gill's contemporaries, Goudy had become a type designer after an earlier career as a lettering artist for advertisers and their agents. So, too, had Ashley Havinden and one or two other designers in England. The same was true of A. M. Cassandre, Maximilien Vox, Marcel Jacno and their contemporaries. In Germany, Behrens, Renner, Erbar, Ehmcke and others became designers of types after typefounding had become important in post-First War industrial Germany, resurgent and clamorous for new markets. The Germans were designers escaping from a long imprisonment in black letter, fulfilling, in vigorous fashion, the hopes which had prompted Count Kessler to found his Cranach Press forty years earlier.

Amongst these designers, the Germans set the pace. With one or two notable exceptions, they seemed to gaze upon the roman alphabet with innocent – some might say, almost demoniacally innocent – eyes. The letter-forms in the types they designed were always novel, frequently improbable, occasionally frightening. Although they were designing the alphabets mainly for export to nations reared on the roman alphabet, there was little in their designs that showed allegiance to the models of earlier Italian, Dutch and English masters. Novelty was their god and

*Published by the Limited Editions Club of New York 1936. Printed by Hague and Gill at Pigotts, High Wycombe.

ABCDEFGHIJK
LMNOPQRST
UVWXYZ

Monotype Floriated Initials *Series 4 3 1*

export markets their objective. Professor Rudolf Koch and E. R. Weiss were almost the only two German designers who had started their careers with a professional interest in alphabets and lettering. Each would essay traditional effects from time to time, but the final results were invariably lettering novelties, frequently of great charm, but prompted and backed by the skilful marketing organizations of the Bauer and Klingspor type foundries. Weiss tried hard with a wide range of traditional letter-forms, but his divagations were too mannered to place them amongst the classic roman type faces.

Seen against the designs of these lively contemporaries, Gill's alphabets, outside the range of his sans serif extravaganzas, seem unusually serene. His true pleasure lay in unceasing revision of those letter-forms he had derived remotely from Rome, directly from Johnston, and, then, by personal adaptation, made his own. His pleasure lay in refining, not in reshaping the classical alphabet, in varying the distribution of weight, the curve of serif, the careful balance of ascender and descender. He was interested in evolving an alphabet that would perhaps be new but never novel. Only in one venture did he show that as a designer of decorative alphabets, suitable for typographical display, he was not inferior to Koch.

In 1929 Gill had designed a floriated initial N for use in the *Perpetua* specimen that was included in the fifth column of *The Fleuron*. Stanley Morison was delighted with the letter and asked him to design an alphabet containing this floriated motif. At that time Gill held that the mechanical methods which the Corporation must employ to reproduce their types contradicted the nature of his design. Hence he declined. In 1936, however, he changed his mind and offered the Monotype Corporation the drawings from which the charming *Floriated Initials* were cut. There have been few happier after-thoughts by a designer. The initials are as delightful as the decorated *Locarno* designs by Rudolf Koch. Unfortunately, they have been but rarely used in England, a strange neglect, for they are well suited to many forms of typographical display, from dust wrappers to occasional items in jobbing printing. The type has been seen in one or two private press books, notably in Evelyn Waugh's editing of Monsignor Ronald Knox's *Sermons*, published by the Dropmore Press in 1951.

Gill dated his final designs as a *Hebrew* and an *Arabic*, both in 1937. In ten years he had designed eleven types, apart from the Gill variants. *Perpetua*, mainly because of its masterly design but partly, perhaps, because of Morison's equally masterly handling of the designer and his designs, is one of the few types of this century which may possibly find some users in the next; *Gill Sans* brought orderliness to what had previously been little more than a typographical shambles; and, in *Joanna*, Gill evolved a typographical masterpiece, which remains virtually unknown and unused.

Recorded thus, Gill's contribution to typographical history may seem slight, but all who deal with the vast and uneven material available to printers and designers will know that the contribution was impressive, unique in our time.

EXPLICIT

Design for final volume of *The Fleuron* (VII. 1930) showing signs of Gill's slab serif structure seen in his later *Solus* and *Joanna* types.